Earl Monroe

THE STORY OF THE NEW YORK KNICKS

Evan Fournier

A HISTORY OF HOOPS

THE STORY OF THE

NEW YORK KNICKS

JIM WHITING

Willis Reed

CREATIVE EDUCATION / CREATIVE PAPERBACKS

Published by Creative Education and Creative Paperbacks
P.O. Box 227, Mankato, Minnesota 56002
Creative Education and Creative Paperbacks are imprints of
The Creative Company
www.thecreativecompany.us

Design and production by Blue Design (www.bluedes.com)
Art direction by Rita Marshall

Photographs by Corbis (Craig Lassig, Jim Young), Getty (Tom Berg, Andrew D.
Bernstein, Bettmann, Jim Cummins, Lachlan Cunningham, James Drake, Focus
On Sport, FPG, Alex Goodlett, Stan Honda, John Iacono, George Long, Andy
Lyons, Jim McIsaac, Fernando Medina, Manny Millan, NBA Photo Library, Doug
Pensinger, Ken Regan, Wen Roberts, Sarah Stier), © Steve Lipofsky, Newscom
(Ting Shen/Xinhua/Photoshot), USPresswire (David Butler II)

Library of Congress Cataloging-in-Publication Data
Names: Whiting, Jim, 1943- author.
Title: The story of the New York Knicks / by Jim Whiting.
Description: Mankato, Minnesota : Creative Education and Creative
   Paperbacks, 2023. | Series: Creative Sports: A History of Hoops |
   Includes index. | Audience: Ages 8-12 |
   Audience: Grades 4-6 | Summary: "Middle grade basketball fans are
   introduced to the extraordinary history of NBA's New York Knicks with a
   photo-laden narrative of their greatest successes and losses"-- Provided
   by publisher.
Identifiers: LCCN 2022016893 (print) | LCCN 2022016894 (ebook) | ISBN
   9781640026360 (library binding) | ISBN 9781682771921 (paperback) | ISBN
   9701640007772 (pdf)
Subjects: LCSH: New York Knickerbockers (Basketball
   team)--History--Juvenile literature. | Basketball--New York (State)--New
   York--History--Juvenile literature.
Classification: LCC GV885.52.N4 W553 2023 (print) | LCC GV885.52.N4
   (ebook) | DDC 796.323/64097471--dc23/eng/20220505
LC record available at https://lccn.loc.gov/2022016893
LC ebook record available at https://lccn.loc.gov/2022016894

Amar'e Stoudemire

CONTENTS

LEGENDS OF THE HARDWOOD

Allan Houston

HOUSTON, WE DON'T HAVE A PROBLEM

Hardly anyone gave the New York Knicks a chance against the Miami Heat in the first round of the 1999 National Basketball Association (NBA) Eastern Conference playoffs. The Heat had the top seed. The Knicks barely squeezed in as the eighth and final seed. Only one 8-seed had ever defeated the top seed in the first round. The Knicks astounded the league with two blowout wins in the first and third games. Miami easily won games 2 and 4.

The decisive Game 5 was a defensive struggle. With 4.5 seconds remaining and Miami ahead 77–76, Knicks shooting guard Allan Houston took an inbounds pass at the top of the key. He dribbled once to muscle his way between two defenders, then launched an off-balance, 10-foot, one-handed shot. The clock showed 0.8 seconds. The ball hit the front rim, caromed high off the backboard, then fell through the net.

Nearly 15,000 Heat fans were shocked into silence. Houston raced around the court before being mobbed by his teammates. "We've lost a lot of games on last-second shots," said Knicks' dominant center Patrick Ewing. "It was finally sweet to be reversed, where we would finally win one."

The Knicks were just getting started. They swept the Atlanta Hawks in the second round. Next up was the conference finals against the second-seeded

LEGENDS
OF THE HARDWOOD

MAKING HISTORY

Nat Clifton was a high school sensation in
Chicago. He was nicknamed "Sweetwater"
because he loved drinking soda pop. Sometimes
he mixed sugar and water. He served in the
army during World War II. After the war he
played for the Harlem Globetrotters. In May
1950, the Knicks made him the first black
athlete to sign a pro basketball contract.
During one game, a rival player yelled a racial
slur. Clifton knocked him unconscious. He never
had that problem again. "Around Chicago and
in the army, I was used to playing with white
players, and I could get along," he said. "They
[the Knicks] were a great bunch of guys."
Clifton averaged 10 points and 8 rebounds a
game during his career.

Nat "Sweetwater" Clifton

Indiana Pacers. The teams split the first two games. The Knicks had another miraculous moment in Game 3. They were down by three points with five seconds left. Power forward Larry Johnson was fouled in the act of sinking a three-point shot. He converted the free throw to give New York a 92–91 victory. The teams split the next two games. Houston dropped 32 points on the Pacers in Game 6 as the Knicks pulled away in the final quarter for a 90–82 series-clinching victory. For the first—and still only–time in NBA history, an 8-seed would play for the NBA championship!

The team dates back to 1946. New York joined the newly formed Basketball Association of America (BAA). Naming the team was easy. "We all put a name in a hat, and when we pulled them out, most of them said Knickerbockers," said team official Fred Podesta. The name referred to early Dutch settlers. They wore pants called knickerbockers. They were rolled up to just below the knees. The name was too long to fit into newspaper headlines. It was quickly shortened to Knicks.

The Knicks went 33–27 in their first season. But they lost in the second round of the playoffs. Respected local coach Joe Lapchick took over. The Knicks compiled

winning marks in the next two seasons. The BAA merged with the National Basketball League (NBL) in 1949 to form the NBA. Even though no starter was taller than 6-foot-6, the Knicks did well. "Everyone knew his role," said center Harry Gallatin. "We played true team ball." The Knicks advanced to the Eastern Division finals in the 1949–50 season. They played in the NBA Finals the next three seasons. They lost each time.

REED TO THE RESCUE

Lapchick retired during the 1955–56 season. His exit started a long period of decline. In the next 10 years, the Knicks only had one winning record. A highlight came in the 1964–65 season. Center Willis Reed won the NBA Rookie of the Year award. He was big enough to mix it up with his fellow big men inside and had the ability to move away from the basket and hit 15-foot jump shots. Reed couldn't win games by himself, though. The team continued to struggle.

The Knicks hired William "Red" Holzman as coach in the middle of the 1967–68 season. He especially emphasized defense. In his first full season, New York won a franchise-best 54 games. But the Knicks lost to the Boston Celtics in the division finals.

The team fired on all cylinders in 1969–70. Holzman had added forwards Dave DeBusschere and Bill Bradley. Point guard Walt "Clyde" Frazier directed the team's offense. The Knicks surged to a 60–22 mark. "Playing basketball [under Holzman]

Willis Reed

became more fun than I had ever imagined," said Bradley. They met the Lakers in the NBA Finals. The Lakers had three superstars: center Wilt Chamberlain, guard Jerry West, and forward Elgin Baylor. The Knicks fought tooth and nail to force the series to seven games.

Reed tore a thigh muscle in Game 5. He sat out Game 6. Without his defensive pressure, Chamberlain torched the Knicks for 45 points to even the series. As the teams warmed up for Game 7, Reed was nowhere in sight. He hobbled onto the court just before the game started. The fans in Madison Square Garden went absolutely and totally bonkers. Reed scored his team's first two baskets. They were his only points. He focused on guarding Chamberlain. Reed's teammates rode the emotional high from his presence. They bolted out to a 61–37 lead before the pain became too great for Reed to continue. They won 113–99.

Bill Bradley

WILLIS REED
POWER FORWARD/CENTER
HEIGHT: 6-FOOT-10
KNICKS SEASONS: 1964–74

A DOMINANT DEFENDER

Willis Reed was born in a Louisiana town that he joked "was so small it didn't even have a population." He led his high school team to state championships in both basketball and football. He could have played either sport at Grambling University. He chose hoops. He got a teaching degree but abandoned the classroom for the hardwood when the Knicks drafted him. He became the team's first-ever NBA Rookie of the Year and was a cornerstone of the defensive-minded Knicks teams of the late 1960s and early 1970s. In 1970, he led New York to its first-ever NBA title while becoming the first player to sweep the MVP awards: regular season, Finals, and All-Star Game. He will always be remembered for his gritty performance during the 1970 Finals. "He can barely walk and we asked him to run," said teammate Cazzie Russell.

NEW YORK KNICKS

LEGENDS OF THE HARDWOOD

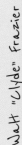
Walt "Clyde" Frazier

WALT "CLYDE" FRAZIER
POINT GUARD
HEIGHT: 6-FOOT-4
KNICKS SEASONS: 1967–77

CLOTHES MAKE THE MAN

Walt Frazier made the All-NBA First Team four times. Teammate Willis Reed praised his leadership qualities. "It's Clyde's ball," Reed said. "He just lets us play with it once in a while." That "Clyde" nickname is one of the NBA's most famous. It came from the gangster movie *Bonnie and Clyde*, which had been released during Frazier's rookie season. The notorious outlaw Clyde Barrow, played by actor Warren Beatty, was a stylish dresser. So was Frazier. He liked to wear full-length mink coats, broad-brimmed fedora hats, and custom-tailored suits. A Knicks' trainer nicknamed him "Clyde." He has been part of the Knicks's broadcasting team for many years and is still a fashion icon. "When I go to a tailor, I say, 'Show me something you think nobody would ever wear,'" he said.

That gave them the NBA championship. "Willis provided the inspiration, I provided the devastation," said Frazier. He scored a game-high 36 points.

The Knicks reached the Eastern Conference finals in 1970–71, then lost the NBA Finals to the Lakers the following season. There was no stopping them in the 1972–73 season. The Knicks trounced the Lakers, 4 games to 1, to win the NBA championship again. It was their second title in four years. "The Knicks are so well-balanced," Chamberlain said, "and have tremendous passing and so many good shooters that you can't concentrate on one man."

New York hoped for a repeat championship in 1974. They advanced to the Eastern Conference finals. They lost to Boston, 4 games to 1. Reed retired. Without him, the Knicks fell to 40–42 in 1974–75. It was their first losing mark in eight years.

THE EWING ERA BEGINS

t seemed obvious that the Knicks needed new blood. But team officials made one of the worst decisions in franchise history before the 1976–77 season. The rival American Basketball Association (ABA) had stopped playing. The New York Nets were one of four ABA teams that joined the NBA. Each team had to pay a $3.2 million entry fee. On top of that, the Knicks claimed that the Nets were "invading" their territory. They demanded that the Nets pay them $4.8 million on top of the entry fee. The Nets offered Julius "Dr. J." Erving to the Knicks instead. Erving was a prolific scorer especially noted for his crowd-pleasing dunks. The Knicks said no. The Philadelphia 76ers bought his contract. Philadelphia advanced to the NBA Finals four times before Dr. J. retired in 1987. He ended his 11-year NBA career with more than 18,000 points (combining both leagues, he had 30,000). During that same time frame, the Knicks had seven losing seasons. They did advance to the conference semifinals three times before bowing out. Two defeats came from the 76ers and Dr. J.

Much of the Knicks' limited success was due to small forward Bernard King. He joined the team in 1982. "He's like a bird," said coach Hubie Brown. "He swoops toward the basket and seems to be descending. Then, at the last instant, he elevates, and you'll see an incredible move." King led the league in scoring in 1984–85. He averaged nearly 33 points a game. Unfortunately, he suffered a severe knee injury late that season. The Knicks finished 24–58. It was their worst record in more than 20 years.

Then the Knicks benefited from some good luck. Teams that didn't qualify for the playoffs held a drawing. The winner had the first choice in the 1985 NBA Draft. There was no question who that choice would be: Patrick Ewing. "Not since Lew Alcindor [later Kareem Abdul-Jabbar] left UCLA in 1969 had there been a giant as dominant as the 7-foot, 240-pound Ewing," said sportswriter Chris Ballard. "He offered the total package. He could score in the post, defend, rebound, and knock down an 18-foot jumper." Ewing also had a scowling "game face" that often intimidated his opponents. The Knicks won the drawing! Ewing averaged 20 points and 9

Bernard King

PATRICK EWING
CENTER
HEIGHT: 7-FOOT-0
KNICKS SEASONS: 1985–2000

THE HEIGHT OF INGRATITUDE

Growing up in Jamaica, Patrick Ewing played cricket and soccer. After moving to Massachusetts at the age of 12, he began playing basketball. He learned the sport quickly. In his senior year at Georgetown University, he was named College Player of the Year. The Knicks made him their top choice in the 1985 NBA Draft. He became an 11-time All-Star and established team records in categories such as points, rebounds, and blocked shots. No one worked harder, both on and off the court. In 2021, he was named one of the 75 greatest players in NBA history. Yet especially near the end of his career, home fans booed him. The Knicks hadn't won a championship during that time. They blamed Ewing. That was unfair. He led the team to 13 straight playoff appearances. In the 10 years after he left, the Knicks had just one winning season and two playoff appearances.

rebounds a game and was named NBA Rookie of the Year. The Knicks won only 23 games in the 1985–86 season. The losing continued in the next two seasons. But things were about to get better.

A RUN OF SUCCESS

New York added point guard Mark Jackson in the 1987 NBA Draft. He averaged nearly 14 points and 11 assists a game. He was named NBA Rookie of the Year. Adding other players such as bruising power forward/center Charles Oakley helped the Knicks become a regular in the playoffs. Another important addition was legendary coach Pat Riley. He won four NBA titles with the Lakers in the 1980s. "The Knicks would never be the Lakers, but by unleashing the snarling talents of guys like [power forward Anthony] Mason and [shooting guard John] Starks, Riley got them good fast," said sportswriter Mark Kriegel. "What they lacked in talent, they made up in heart, hustle, and hard work."

The Knicks reached the NBA Finals in 1994. They took a 3–2 series lead over the Houston Rockets. They didn't shoot well in the next two games. They had a hard time getting the ball inside to Ewing. The Rockets won both games and the title. By that time, Riley wanted more power over personnel decisions and more money than the team was willing to give him. He moved on to coach the Miami Heat after the 1994–95 season.

1994 NBA Finals

The Knicks continued to play well after Riley left. They made it to the conference semifinals the next three seasons. Most people didn't think much of the team's chances in the lockout-shortened 1998–99 season. New York went just 27–23 and barely qualified for the playoffs. Everything seemed to come together as they romped through the playoffs before meeting the San Antonio Spurs for the championship. But both Ewing and Larry Johnson missed the series due to injuries. New York was no match for the Spurs. San Antonio took the series, 4 games to 1.

The Knicks reached the Eastern Conference finals the following year. Again, they faced Indiana. The Pacers took the series. Team officials decided they couldn't win the championship with Ewing. They traded him. "Patrick is a champion, even if he hasn't won a championship yet," said coach Jeff Van Gundy. "He practiced and played like a champion each day he was here."

Carmelo Anthony

A LONG SHOT SCORES A BULLSEYE

John Starks wasn't drafted after playing college basketball. He signed with the Golden State Warriors but hardly ever got off the bench. He tried out for the Knicks before the 1990 season. During a practice, he tried to dunk over Patrick Ewing. Ewing knocked him down and Starks twisted a knee. Under league rules, the team couldn't release him until it healed. They planned on cutting him at that point. But by then, another guard had been injured. That created a roster opening for Starks. He took full advantage of it. He immediately became an important part of the rotation coming off the bench. Two years later, he became a starter. He averaged 14 points a game during his Knicks career. His 982 three-point field goals were a Knicks all-time record for more than 20 seasons.

JOHN STARKS
SHOOTING GUARD
HEIGHT: 6-FOOT-3
KNICKS SEASONS: 1990–98

A LONG DRY SPELL

ew York didn't play like champions after Ewing's departure. They did win 48 games in 2000–01. But they lost in the first round of the playoffs. They tumbled to 30 wins the following season. It was the first time in 15 years that they hadn't qualified for the playoffs. That began a series of trades that confused fans and led to steady losses. New York didn't have a winning record for the next eight seasons. They continued to trade for expensive players who didn't produce on the court.

The Knicks signed All-Star center/power forward Amar'e Stoudamire before the 2010–11 season. "We have taken a big step with Amar'e and we will take another big step, whether that is today or tomorrow or six months from now," said coach Mike D'Antoni. "Another big step" came a few months later. New York made a blockbuster trade for superstar forward Carmelo Anthony. "Carmelo is in the prime of his NBA career having already established himself as a one of the game's elite players," said Knicks president Donnie Walsh. The Knicks had winning records for the next three years. The 2011–12 season was highlighted by point/shooting guard Jeremy Lin and "Linsanity." The Knicks advanced to the Eastern Conference semifinals in 2013. They lost to the Pacers.

The Knicks won only 37 games in 2013–14. The wheels came off the following season. The Knicks had a franchise-worst 17–65 record. The team won 32 games in 2015–16 as 7-foot-3 rookie power forward Kristaps Porziṅgis made an impressive debut. He averaged 14 points, 7 rebounds, and 2 blocked shots a game.

LEGENDS
OF THE HARDWOOD

LINSANITY

The Houston Rockets cut Jeremy Lin on Christmas Eve 2011. The Knicks signed him three days later. No one expected much. He hardly played for more than a month. Coach Mike D'Antoni finally gave Lin more playing time on February 4. He scored 25 points. He netted 28 in the next game, then 23, then 38. The Knicks won all four games. A few days later, Lin sank a desperation three-point shot to win yet another game. Metta World Peace of the Lakers watched the game. He screamed "Linsanity! Linsanity!" as he ran by reporters. The name stuck. It was a combination of Lin's last name and "insanity." After the season, Lin returned to the Rockets. He left the NBA in 2019 and currently plays in China.

R.J. Barrett

The additions didn't help. The Knicks won just 31 and 29 games in the next two seasons. Porziņģis tore his Achilles tendon late in the 2017–18 season. He missed all of the following season as the Knicks won just 17 games. In the COVID-19 shortened 2019–20 season, New York won only 21 games. The team fell far short of the playoffs.

After a slow start in 2020–21, the Knicks finished with a 16–4 record. It was keyed by second-year shooting guard R.J. Barrett and NBA Most Improved Player power forward Julius Randle. Their 41–31 mark was the first winning record in eight seasons. Unfortunately, they lost to Atlanta in the first round of the playoffs. New York appeared to maintain their momentum as they won five of their first six games in 2021–22. They were still at .500 just past the halfway point of the season. But the Knicks won just one game in February. They fell out of playoff contention. Several of those losses came after the Knicks blew double-digit leads. New York will look to return to postseason following the off-season signing of guard Jalen Brunson. He had his best season to date in 2021-22. He averaged over 16 points and nearly 5 assists per game for the Dallas Mavericks.

The New York Knicks have a long and distinguished history. They have had an interesting pattern of wins and losses. They did well in odd-numbered decades: 1950s, 1970s, and 1990s. The pattern continued at the start of 2010s, with three straight playoff appearances. But seven losing seasons followed. Fans hope the team will return to its previous winning form and add another championship banner to the rafters of Madison Square Garden.

Julius Randle

INDEX